the Misphits

PRESENT

Carma'stail

DIARY OF A
HOMELESS ALBINO
PIT BULL

THE AUTHORS OF the Misphits · BOOK DESIGN BY MARK TAYLOR

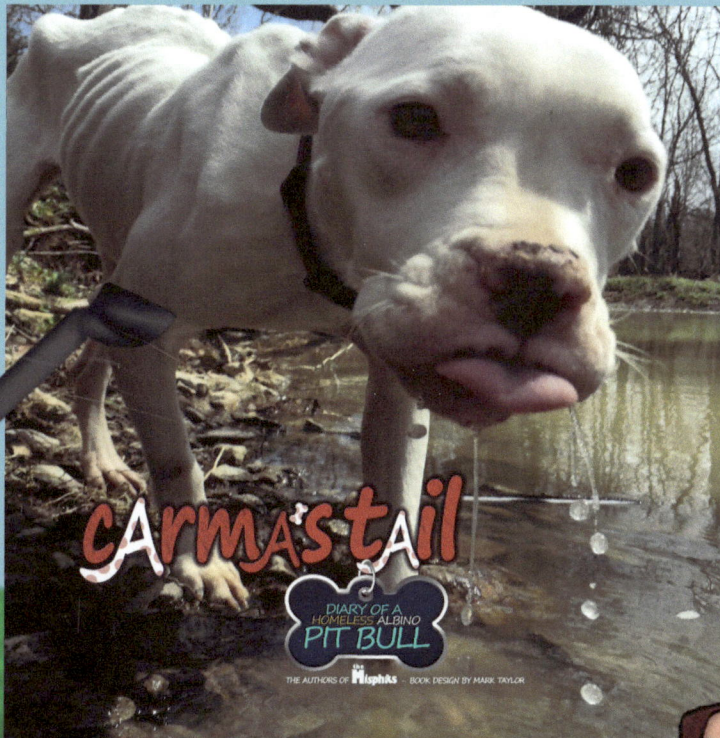

Carmastail.com
@carmastail / #carmastail
Misphits.com

Shamrock Pet Foundation, Inc.
A lifelong loving home for every pet.

Mission:
To enhance the lives of companion animals through
proactive programs such as spay/neuter,
public education and adoption options.

100% of the profits from this book will go to the
Shamrock Pet Foundation to help other animals just like Carma!

For more information and some of our success stories,
please see the back of this book or visit
ShamrockPets.com

This book is dedicated to humans that save and
love all animals...and our moms

It is our hope that Carma's diary
entertains, educates and encourages more
animal rescues. Enjoy!

DAY 63

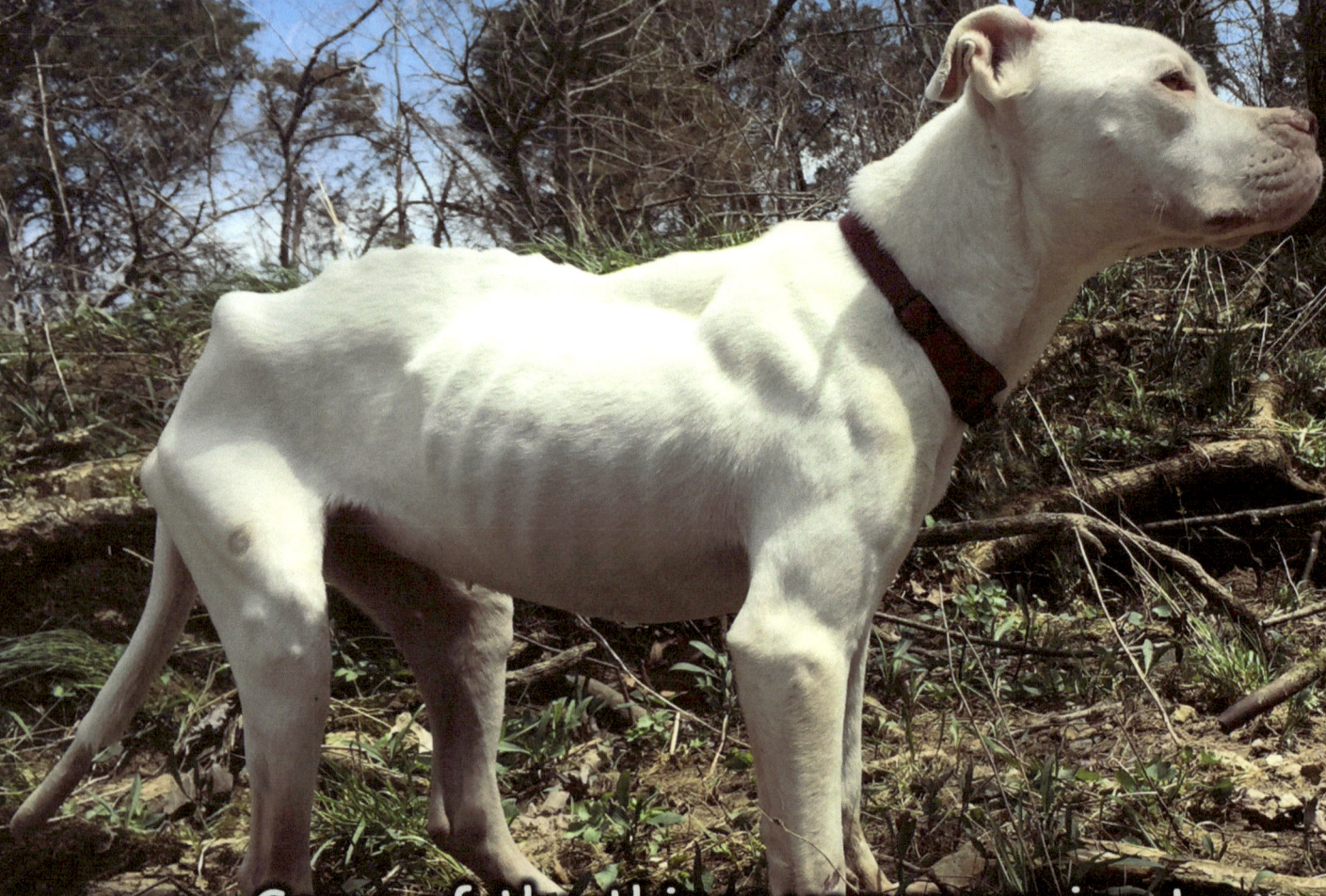

Some of the things you are going to learn from my diary may seem hard to believe, but everything you are about to read is based on a true tale.

1

I've been out here alone for a really long time and I'm starting to lose hope that my master will ever find me.
I'm lonely, weak, starving...

Weight of 31 lbs

...and I don't remember the last time I felt safe.

There are three things you NEED to survive:

food, shelter and water...

and right now, I only have muddy creek water. I hope something changes soon.

As I laid in the morning sun trying to get warm, I suddenly smelled something very familiar but almost forgotten. I slowly stood up and saw a man carefully walking towards me.

He began to speak very softly, went down on one knee and reached out to let me sniff his hand.

He smelled soooooooooooo good, I rolled over and began to wag my tail.

My heart got warm as he gently rubbed my belly.

After petting me for a while, the man stood up, reached in his pocket and fed me some almonds.

8

He asked me to follow him into his car. I hadn't been in one of these since my master and I lost each other. I didn't know what was happening, but anything was better than being cold and alone.

As we were driving, he called me

Carma.

10

WHAT TO DO IF YOU FIND OR SEE A LOST DOG?

CAN I HELP?

NO →

PET SHELTER

Call your local animal shelter, humane society, veterinarian or animal welfare organization with the exact location of the dog. If possible, stay with the dog until help arrives.

YES ↓

NO

Approach dog slowly and with caution. Be sure to speak gently and approach with hand out flat.

Is the dog's tail wagging or is it rolling over to ask you to pet its belly?

YES

YES →

See if you can get financial aid or discount from vet. Talk to the vet about parasites, vaccinations, proper diet and proper medical care. Prepare your home and mind. Leave your contact information in case the owner contacts the vet.

Take dog to vet and check for microchipping.

If the dog does not have a microchip, do I have the time, money, space and proper environment to temporarily take the dog home until the owner can be found?

NO →

Call your local no-kill shelter or animal welfare organization and arrange to drop the dog off.

NO ↑

If dog seems friendly, gently pet it and check for tags. Does the dog have tags with owner info?

Contact owner and stay with dog until owner arrives

YES →

We drove for a while, then the man took me to a place that smelled like a whole lot of animals. Smiling faces greeted us, put medicine on my boo boos and told the man how to take care of me. I was happy when the man said "come Carma" and motioned for me to follow him out the door.

The car slowed down and we pulled up to a house with lots of land. We got out of his car and I was introduced one by one to three dogs and four girls. It had been a big day so I was happy when the man took me to my own room with a bowl of food, fresh water and a warm bed!

DAY 64 - Day 77

Even though I'm feeling better, I'm still really tired and hungry. As hungry as I am though, I get sick if I eat too much food all at once.

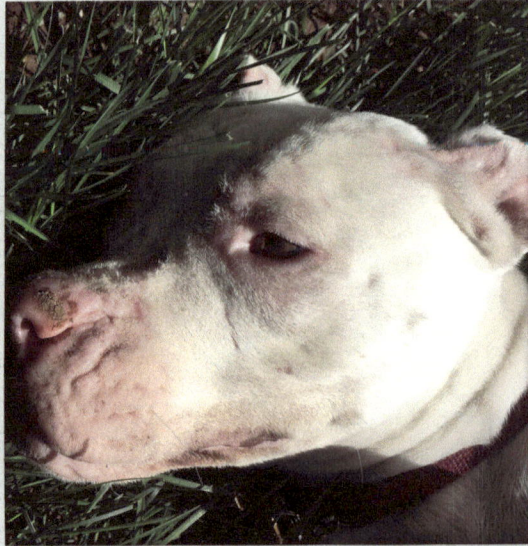

Weight of 42 lbs

The family also started potty training me, but I surprised them because I already knew I needed to go outside.

They are also helping me remember my manners.

Day 78

It's been two weeks since the man found me, but it's still a bumpy road to recovery.

My fur is falling out, my boo boos are just now beginning to heal and I still have a lot of belly aches.

AM I ABLE TO ADOPT A DOG?

Start at **1**. Read the question and if you answer YES, draw a line to the next number. If NO, skip to the next number.

Is everybody in my family ok with adopting a dog and is everybody dog allergy-free?

1

Do we have time to potty train, exercise, cuddle and teach manners?

CARMA

If I have other animals in my house, will they be ok with a dog visiting?

5

2

Does our home have enough space for a dog, including a place that she can eat and sleep alone?

4

3

Do we have the money to pay for food, vet visits, spaying or neutering and medicine?

If your dog house is complete, congratulations, you are ready to adopt. If not, adoption is not right for you at this time, but you can still volunteer at a shelter. Please move on to the next page.

Do I know how to make a dog healthy and keep it safe?

A How many dogs should I introduce to the new dog at one time?
- one
- two
- three

B When should I let the dog have water?
- once a day
- twice a day
- all day long

C If the dog is four years old, what type of food should it eat?
- bacon and eggs
- adult dog food
- puppy food

D Is it ok to leave the new dog unattended and unsupervised when you leave your house?
- yes
- no

(A) one   (B) all day long   (C) adult dog food   (D) no

What type of dog would be right for me?

SIZE
- LARGE
- MEDIUM
- SMALL

TEMPERMENT
- FRIENDLY WITH EVERYONE
- COMFORTABLE WITH JUST MY FAMILY

FUR
- LONG
- SHORT

ENERGY
- RUN & PLAY
- CUDDLE & SLEEP

TRAINING
- LOVES TO TRAIN
- HAPPY WITH JUST SIT AND STAY

Look at me! My fur has grown back, I'm gaining weight and my belly has stopped hurting.

Day 92

It's amazing how much better I feel when I eat good food every day. I finally have the energy to explore.

My manners are now so much better that I'm being allowed to roam the house whenever I want and I can even sleep on the couch! I'm happy we're all feeling more comfortable.

NIGHT 95

These are some pictures of my new BFF, Lola. We had our first playdate late at night and now we have them all the time. She is soooo much fun!

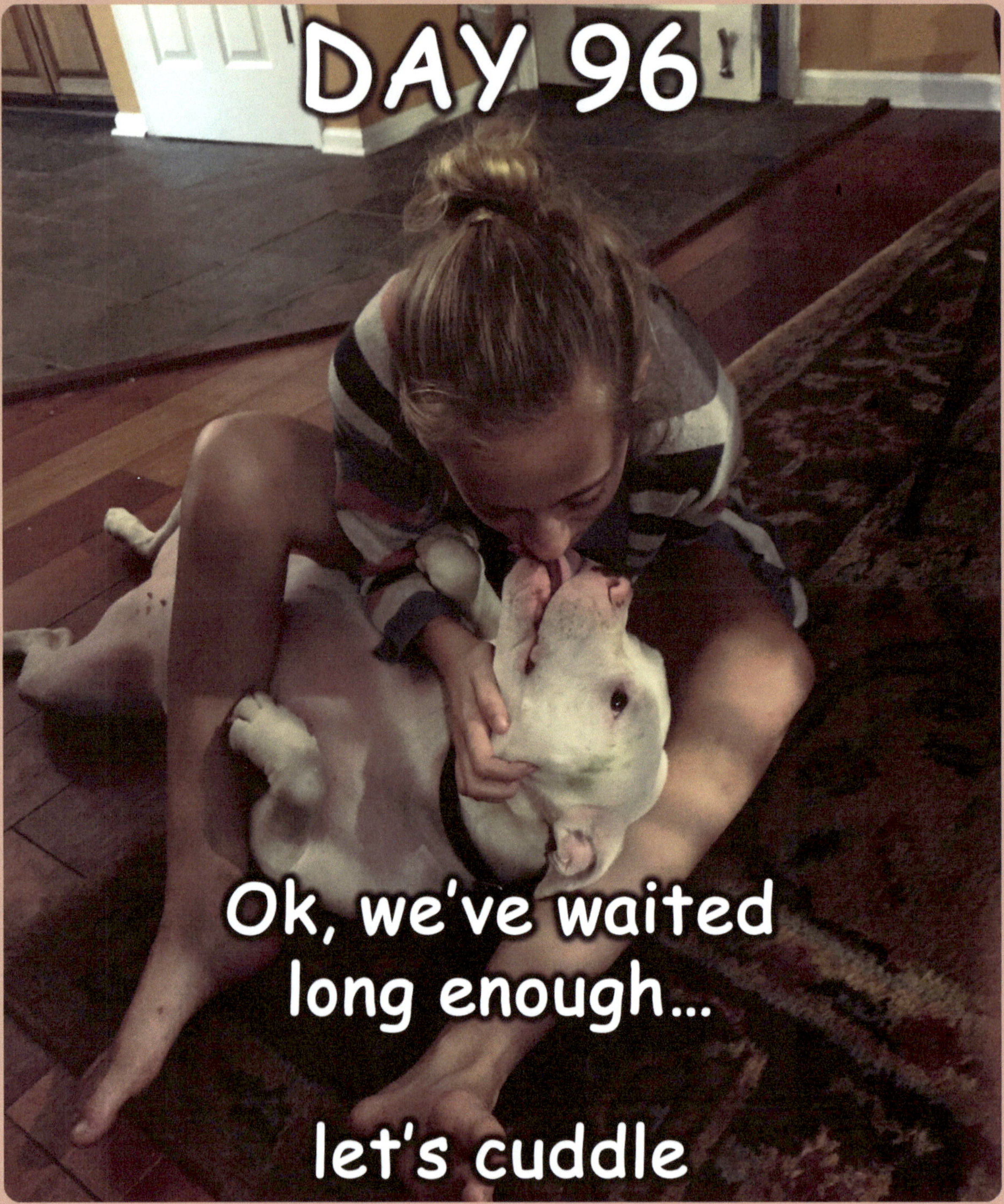
DAY 96
Ok, we've waited
long enough...
let's cuddle

I think I may have a new family.

WHAT IF CARMA IS NOT A GOOD FIT FOR OUR HOME?

Not everybody can take in every animal that is rescued and some people are in a position where they can't have an animal at all (allergies, no space, or no money).

If you are unable to have a pet, what are some other things you can do to help animals in your community?

DONATE

ATTEND AN ANIMAL EDUCATION CAMP

FUNDRAISE

VOLUNTEER

If you answered **ALL OF THESE** stand up, howl and wag your tail because all these things improve the lives of animals.

Which of these items would be helpful if they were donated to an animal shelter?

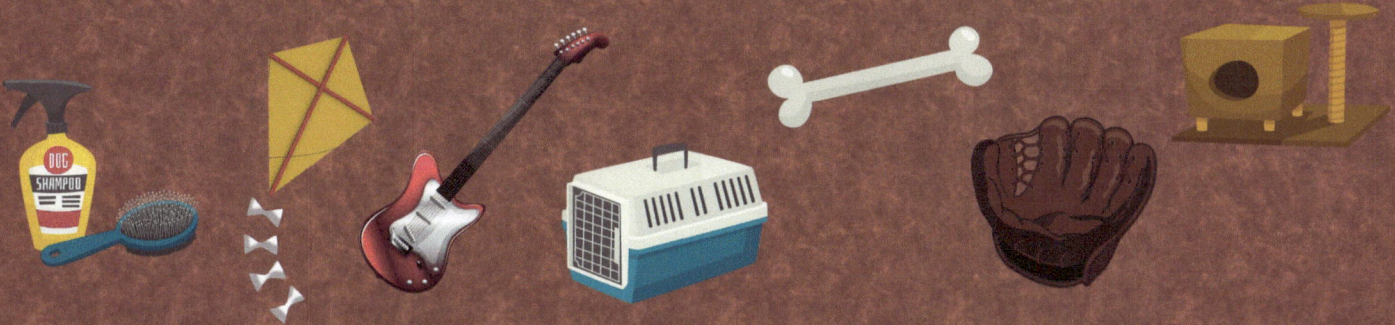

Can you please list some things you might learn at a
Humane Organization Animal Camp?

Do you know whom you should call if you find a
lost, hurt or abused animal?

Research and list three rescue groups or shelters in your area.
Write their names and websites below.

1.

2.

3.

DAY 97

It's OFFICIAL!!!

I have a new family and a forever home!

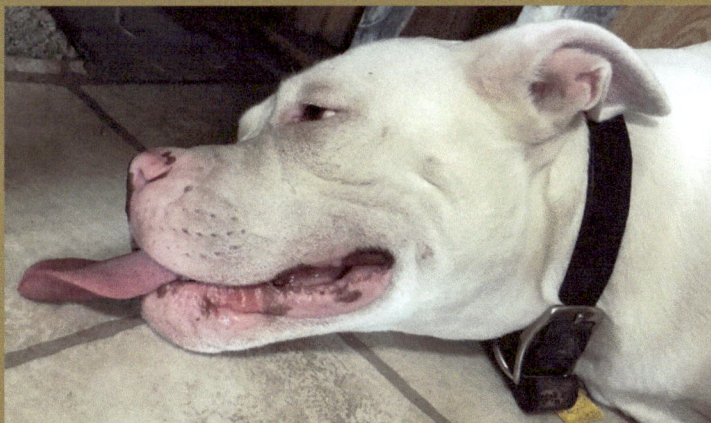

...and every day is a new adventure

DAY 98

I am very thankful...

31

I was rescued by my family and am so happy to spend the rest of my life in my new home. We love each other so much and they take such good care of me.

I'm one lucky pup.

Even though it wasn't easy, the one thing I learned along the way is to never give up even when there seems like there is no way out,

because...

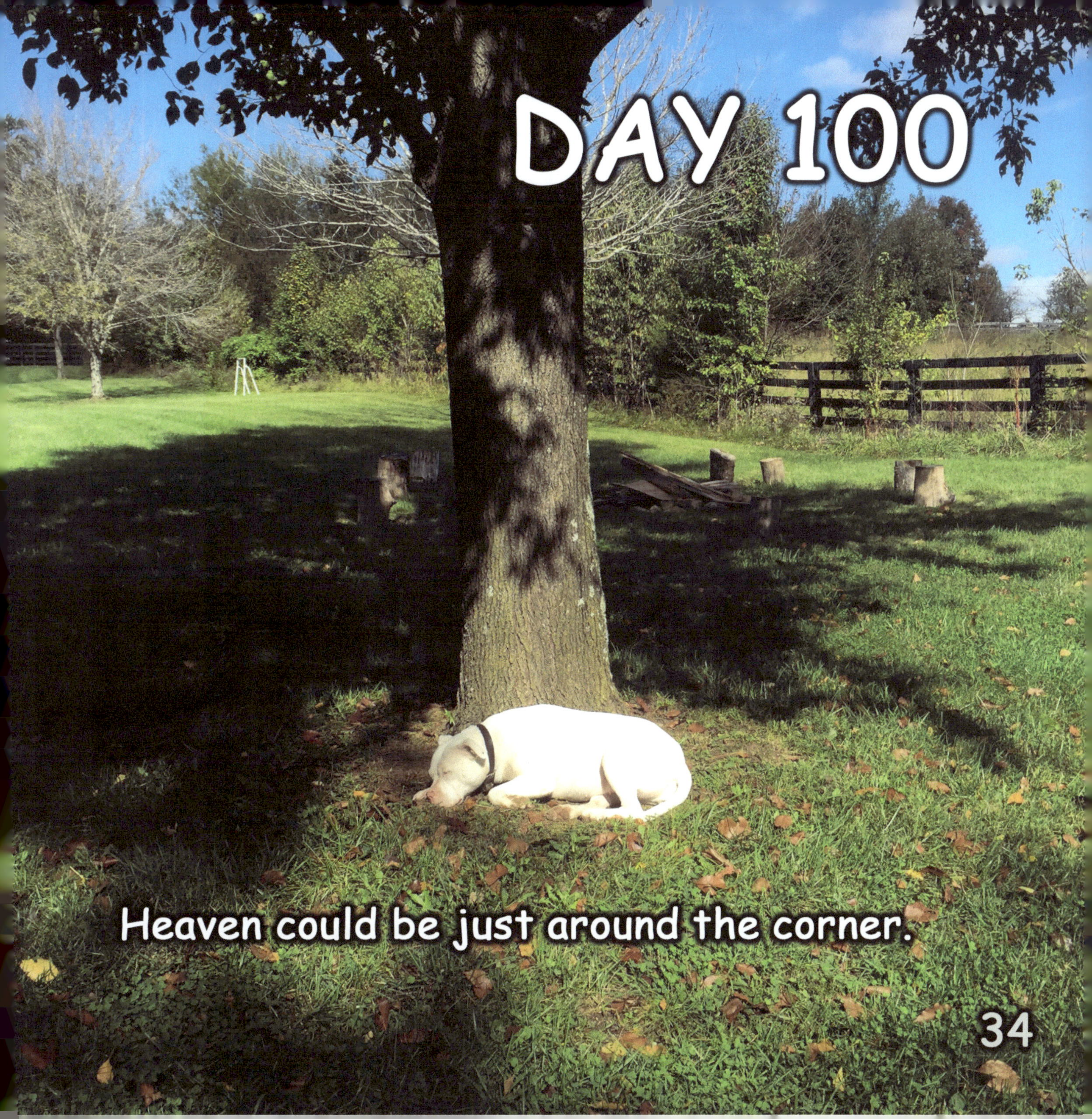

DAY 100

Heaven could be just around the corner.

Shamrock Pet Foundation
A lifelong loving home for every pet.

Since 1992 the Shamrock Pet Foundation's number one priority has been providing spay/neuter assistance for the Kentuckiana area. Spay/neuter decreases the number of unwanted litters thus decreasing the number of puppies, kittens, cats and dogs taken to the already overcrowded shelters and facing euthanasia.

Shamrock, also, provides aid to animals that have been abandoned, injured, abused, found in dumpsters and/or have been victims of neglect. We are sometimes the only or last chance for some of these animals.

Shamrock has helped people who love their pets but find themselves in financial despair with a very ill animal that needs medical attention. We have stepped in providing assistance for these families and pets. For some of these people, their pets are the only family they have, especially the elderly.

Shamrock Pet Foundation is grateful and proud that we were there for Carma and many other animals in terrible, life threatening situations. Here are just a few of our success stories!

Garfield was rescued from the streets showing the effects of being homeless, hungry and sick. Now he is happy, healthy and the "Official Greeter" at one of our local veterinarian offices.

Marley, rescued from a local shelter with a severely injured eye, on his way to the animal hospital for care.

Maddie, a beautiful Chocolate Lab, needed surgery for a torn ACL and could barely walk. After recovering from her surgery she's like a pup again.

If you see an animal that needs your help, please do whatever you can to lend a hand. Be a voice for the voiceless because animals like Carma depend on us.

www.ingramcontent.com/pod-product-compliance
Lightning Source LLC
Chambersburg PA
CBHW041548040426
42447CB00002B/88